Anyone

PHOENIX POETS

NATE KLUG

Anyone

THE UNIVERSITY OF CHICAGO PRESS
Chicago & London

NATE KLUG is the author of *Rude Woods*, a book-length adaptation of Virgil's *Eclogues*. A UCC-Congregationalist minister, he has served churches in North Guilford, Connecticut, and Grinnell, Iowa.

The University of Chicago Press, Chicago 60637
The University of Chicago Press, Ltd., London
© 2015 by The University of Chicago
All rights reserved. Published 2015.
Printed in the United States of America

24 23 22 21 20 19 18 17 16 15   1 2 3 4 5

ISBN-13: 978-0-226-19695-4 (paper)
ISBN-13: 978-0-226-19700-5 (e-book)
DOI: 10.7208/chicago/9780226197005.001.0001

Library of Congress Cataloging-in-Publication Data
Klug, Nate, 1985- author.
    Anyone / Nate Klug.
        pages cm — (Phoenix poets)
    Poems.
    Includes bibliographical references.
        ISBN 978-0-226-19695-4 (paperback : alkaline paper) —
ISBN 978-0-226-19700-5 (e-book)
    I. Title.
    PS3611.L82A84 2015
    811'.6—dc23

                                    2014014263

⊗ This paper meets the requirements of ANSI/NISO Z39.48-1992
(Permanence of Paper).

for MY MOTHER AND FATHER

In the whole that is unnecessary, every small thing becomes necessary....

Thomas Merton (on Louis Zukofsky)

CONTENTS

ACKNOWLEDGMENTS

Thanks to the editors of the following journals:

Common Knowledge: "Predestination," "Three Days"
Free Verse: "Sound from Sound," "Thinking"
Harvard Divinity Bulletin and *NPR.org*: "Mercy"
Poetry: "Advent," "The Choice," "Conjugations," "Dare," "Milton's
    God," "Observer," "Parade," "Squirrels," "True Love," "Work"
Poetry Northwest: "Home," "Neighbors," "Novitiate," "The Truly
    Fucked"
The Threepenny Review: "In Calico Rock, Arkansas"
The Yale Review: Part of "Lost Seasons" as "End of Autumn"
Zoland Poetry: "Errand"

Some of these poems were first collected in a chapbook, *Consent*
(Brooklyn, NY: Pressed Wafer, 2012).

WORK

It hides its edges
in speed, it has
no edges. Plus every time
he thinks he knows

it closely enough—can discriminate
centripetal force
from what gets sheared
straight off—

direction changes:
through stunned space the blade
snaps back,
turtles into its handle,

and starts over spinning
the other way.
All along the chopped-up sidewalk
(the need to keep

breaking what we make
to keep making)
the concrete saw
plunges and resurfaces,

precise as a skull;
it glints against
the small smoke
of its own work.

CONJUGATIONS

This early the garden's bare
but people pay to walk it,

at plots of budless brush
stop, as if remembering,

and stoop to mouth the names—
araucaria

araucana, monkey
puzzle tree, something

Japanese—each particular
ridiculous *to be*.

MILTON'S GOD

Where I-95 meets The Pike,
a ponderous thunderhead flowered—

stewed a minute, then flipped
like a flash card, tattered
edges crinkling in, linings so *dark*
with excessive bright

that, standing, waiting, at the overpass edge,
the onlooker couldn't decide

until the end, or even then,
what was revealed and what had been hidden.

LETTER OF INTRODUCTION,
SAMUEL PALMER TO HIS PATRON

Not a naturalist by profession—
though one does attend the need, now and then,
what could be called compulsion, even,
        of first-rate distances; I mean

    I like the look of light
ruffling mosses and knotgrass, the way
perception rambles to catch upon
        the particular heat of an oak tree's

    barky furrows: a life,
in other words, spent far from the globosities
of Art, and not without its own
        excesses—those shy infrequent glimpses,

    half-returned, of one
of the Tatham girls in town—which straightaway incite
the eyes' darting artilleries
        beneath my spoiled spectacles.

    P.S. Am looking for a wife.

THINKING
(after Virgil, *Aeneid* 8)

News comes from Latium
and now he has to decide; but thinking,
too quick for itself, splits as it starts,
it pours into one plan's form
then jars and recombines, as if
to elaborate his fate from every angle
were to understand it:

                            so the light
held within a copper bowl
of water, shaking back the sun
or a moon's glimmering particles,
will flit and work upon the walls
and crannies in an empty room,
rising to strike the ceiling, trembling,

though both water and bowl are still.

THE CHOICE

To stand sometime
outside my faith

to steady it
caught and squirming on a stick
up to mind's
inviting light

and name it!
for all its faults and facets

or keep waiting

to be claimed in it

DUSK IN JASPER COUNTY

Silos and the animals slowing
almost stumbling
among their shadows

hills fuzzed with a concentration of mist
so pale it cannot be darkness, then it is

as I-80 blinks
and unfolds
dumbly as a sea road

or certain sleeplessness
blank cracked ceiling staring back

at your desire
sick for several lives
and each at once

HOME

Whorl of underpasses, off-ramps,
freeways that splay
running sedans and tanker trucks

to odd-numbered interstates
with Indian names:
everything aiming

at everything
and just missing
in eternal roar and return,

sky fixed with the rickety
circuitry of an old roller coaster park
when we break

out of the airport tunnel—
ascension, assimilation:
even the wish

in the back of a cab not to think
comes with its own
moving pictures and music.

NEIGHBORS

The sounds dawn slowly
on the drifting brain,
steaming up through the flooring and flecked carpet
like an unidentified, but welcome, scent,
from their sources below
gently extending a circumference.
It might start, prolific mornings, around ten.
More often, though, I didn't hear them
until well into the afternoon,
a muffled two-part counterpoint, indistinct at first
from passing subwoofed hip-hop
or the delimber machine, stewing and rattling
several houses down—
                                    how helpless,
how easily betrayed to their true worth
are *the efforts of thought,*
fidgeting among illustrious books
whenever the strangers' familiar sighs rise up.

TO EGNATIUS, WHO WON'T STOP SMILING
(after Catullus)

Picture him on a defendant's bench in Rome:
a lawyer clears his throat,
shuffles folders,
preparing to rework an old tearjerker

while the whole crowd leans in, silent, intent
—except for one Egnatius,
smiling like an idiot,
thinking how white his teeth will appear

to all these people. Or at the funeral home,
paying our respects
to the young dead captain,
a touch on the shoulder and whispered lie

to his sobbing mother—happen to turn
and see Egnatius,
hovering in the corner
by the cheap cheeses: there's that wandering gaze

and shit-eating grin again. Anything could be
going on, anywhere;
Egnatius will be there,
clueless as to his illness, smiling. Short Sabines,

fat Etruscans, Lanuvinians who have black skin,
and those of us native
to Verona, we each keep
our teeth reasonably clean—and hidden.

We've heard, Egnatius, where *you* come from.
And it seems it is the custom
in your Spain, after one awakes
and pisses, to wash out the mouth with one's own urine.

So from now on, whenever you show up at something,
your bared chompers enviably white,
we'll all take it as a sign
you must have drunk an extra cup that morning.

JON'S JOG

At Maspeth Creek, he cuts
his familiar unexpected path
along the old offal docks, dodging wrack
and the yawning delivery truck,
following hunches in a dawn haze

while the drifting grit and airborne
oils, the night soil smell
that never quite left this part of the borough,
begin to work into his skin
like strange fuels, driving him

back up towards the big avenues,
alleys shrugging off shadow now
as a bodega owner unlocks, locks, and unlocks
a stuck grate, until the sallow glare
of the Boar's Head factory reappears,

marking the turn onto his street:
home early, his roommates still asleep,
skin itching with dust and sweat
and the first reckless edges of a fire
which is not change, but may contain it.

ADVENT

In the middle of December
to start over

to assume again
an order

at the end
of wonder

to conjure
and then to keep

slow dirty sleet
within its streetlight

PARADE
Fourth of July, New Hampshire

As with this Jet Ski family
      braiding the lake
with bigger and bigger shocks
until the one
      car-sized one
cuts his engine
and, following him, for an instant
      they all coast
through silences
of self-made
      rain—

      how much violence
is required now
          to carve,
out of the general
livable quiet,
      independence?

A MESSAGE
(after Kafka)

So it runs: the Emperor, on his deathbed,
has a message for you,
humble subject, insignificant shadow.
With his left arm, now his right,
the holy messenger must fight
his way down the palace staircase,
past the coiled snake
of the waiting crowd: soldiers, beggars,
boys on tiptoes—could he reach the open
fields how he would fly, how soon you'd hear
the welcome chatter of fists
at your door. He's cleared
the inner chambers, still has the gardens to cross,
a second outer palace, more stairs,
new set of gardens, an outer palace.
It goes on like this for hundreds of years.
If at last he should limp through
the ultimate gate—never, it can never happen—
he'd see outstretched before him
the imperial capital, center of the world, rustling
with red wine and shit and music.
Here, nobody can make it, least of all
a corpse's courier. But you sit
at your apartment window, whispering
such a story into evening.

LULLABY ON ELECTION EVE

Let the salt night stir
among cinder blocks
and the old Caterpillar plough in the yard,
realty signs unhinged since Irene;

let snow, like a sandstorm
or Operation New Dawn,
cancel the low motel roofs, then the cars,

and prepare less predictable shapes.
No reason for us to have been here,
no messages but in sleep.

LOST SEASONS

I.

Squared into neat fires
edging the lawn,
maple leaves scatter
at the first swell of storm:

pile tops, like tile roofs,
lifted, assumed
into one brief
funneling garland of seed

that lurches above the pavement.
Tomorrow, a fretwork
of muddy leaf prints:
new birds crowding the dark.

2.

Streaked red by woodchips
and stacked contiguous
either side of the curb
like model mountain ranges

or near a drain grate islanded
in a stubborn, clinging scarp:
driveway gravel,
duff, two months of doggy marks

pressed together
until the ridges glitter
with a peeling spray-paint sheen
dry as Styrofoam—

too brittle now to melt
they'll wait, nearer air
each day, then disappear
one warm and sudden rain.

SHIFTS
Bridgeport Hospital, Connecticut

Glassed in behind
the grill station's steam,
she chops and shovels
the daily specials,
calling each woman *mami*,
each man *baby*.

———

Twenty-year-old
shot in stomach, arrived
dead on gurney 1:16 a.m.
The shrinking immaculate room.
And one at his chest
who kept pushing, pushing
as if knocking,
awaiting breath
or the right time to quit.

———

Irish Blessings!
on the new balloons
at Jazzman's Café.
Cards for every sort
of accident and holiday.
43 to 42; 68 degrees.
"Whaddya, havin' a baby?"

———

Schine 7 hallway traffic
eyeless as a city sidewalk:
nurses wrapped around their charting
booths, tuxedoed marching
food service, timid priest.
Then off the hall, behind a door,
through dividing curtain and sheets
her everywhere-audible "fix me
motherfucker fix me."

———

Dying shyly,
a nurses' favorite
juggled his breath
mask, shifted
its pale face
across his face,
deliberating
between competing
concealments.

———

Swiping in, a nurse named Dave
turns his baseball cap around.

IN CALICO ROCK, ARKANSAS
Matthew 26:73

From No Jake Brake
and No Barn Burn

on to Peppersauce
and Greasy Slim

old East Calico
now a ghost town

so anyone's language
shall reveal him

decrepit stones
once City Jail

tells iron sign
the words still welded

kept and lost
in Calico Rock

NOVITIATE

for Matt (Brother Isaac)

Entire Thursdays in your room.
Morning's easy, now afternoon
with its sense of sand leaking
from your fist: holes in prayer
everywhere you'd already filled them.
Breathing out, you think
not of the Psalms but lazy dogs
as sunlight forks and darts
across the floor—ambiguous flashes
of oak roots under water
or, lacunae intact,
a scroll from Qumran,
swallowed by a bunch of passing clouds.
A superior knocks at four,
speaks the sound
of someone else's name,
leaves a small meal by the door.

GIFT

Not easy ever
once you have been shocked

to place your index finger
on exactly the same spot

yet you are compelled,
indulged (by whom?), into

repeating yourself—you
who have been called

THREE DAYS

"this onward trick of nature" —Emerson

I.

Like standing
over a hollowed
bed in the morning
not knowing who
wrested you
from it. Mostly, nothing

2.

Find yourself
finding yourself again
plumbing the river thicket
for a deeper russet
still to build a world with

3.

The loneliness of happiness
the happiness in loneliness
the haplessness

OCTONAIRE ON THE WORLD'S VANITY AND INCONSTANCY

(after Antoine de Chandieu)

When the sky's dark face
catches his eye again,

let memory write
of a darkness beyond this:

days self-blinded, nights
of searching untaught,

thinking his own thought
light.

SOUND FROM SOUND
(after Virgil, *Aeneid* 2)

Swirling, returning through the pines' screen,
the sounds were faint but they kept coming
until the *ping* of battleaxes and men's screams
covered, then became, the silence.
Still rubbing sleep away, I stumbled
out onto the winding gabled roof
of my father's house ...

                         as when a wheat field
explodes in wind-tugged flames, or a freshet,
wedged among low mountain ledges,
building up speed, finally lands
and in an instant the meadow vanishes,
crops are crushed, a whole forest,
uprooted, starts wobbling off—

while the shepherd stands, frozen, picking
sound from sound on a distant rock.

SACRED HARP SING,
BETHEL PRIMITIVE BAPTIST

Tufts of dust dislodge and make to jump
among the floorboard cracks as the tenors,
abetted by a redheaded clan up from San
Antonio, drag their nasal, wavering line
towards the chairless center of the room
where the caller stands and each sung part collides,
like flocks of starlings seething a wider cloud.
Fifty left hands chop at the downbeat
until what began as a sexual moan fills in,
turns, reluctantly, into a tune:
Farewell vain world I'm going home
away to New Jerusalem
and I don't care to stay here long.

Shadowed at the back of the fellowship hall,
the convention secretary sneaks a glance
at her phone; soon they'll break for potato salad,
cold cuts, another chance for Larry
to hawk his T-shirts. But for now,
between #282's final note
and whenever the potluck line succumbs
to small talk—
                          now, despite herself,
she sees it: a sheer tower of sound, tottering,
dissolving, in the hollow of the square.

ANYONE

Though severed from their source,
fireflies at the edge of the yard
retain lightning's silence,

the way one flash can confound
distance, turning the roadside
cornstalks white for a garish moment

while I-80's night trucks
punch past,
bearing John 3:16 and Tyson.

Tonight from a stranger's porch, we watched
the tiny orbs form
from sifting dark,

flittings so regular
they felt elemental, one part
with the air, as though

it were our eyes that flickered,
eventually gave out.
Why, when light

in such compression chooses
to betray itself, does it seem
aimed not at particular

conditioned attentions,
but at anyone,
anyone it pleases?

DARE

Not, this time, to infer
but to wait you out
between regret and parking lot
somewhere in the day
like a dare

Salt grime and the foodcarts'
rising steam, at Prospect St. a goshawk
huge and aloof, picking at something,
nested in twigs and police tape
for a while we all
held our phones up

It is relentless, the suddenness
of every other
song, creature, neighbor
as though this life
would prove you
only by turning into itself

ERRAND

Watchfulness in unexpected fits
like photic sneeze reflex,
this morning the big tree's blown
a horny cauliflower crown,
white petals that come off wetly,
in fistfuls, all down the sidewalk
mid-May's incessant blooming,
shedding, how each eyed thing
refuses sameness, is this praise then?

PREDESTINATION

Watched,
so watching

A helpless slouching, settling in
as on a long train

Clicking by,
a square of sky

The same or changed
clicking by

THE TRULY FUCKED
(after Horace)

Who is that skinny boy trailing musk clouds,
Duane Reade roses in his right hand,
who follows you around
these strobe-lit basement parties, Pyrrha?

While you finger your platinum bangs
and tilt your head to the downbeat,
who is it that you picture
standing behind you off to one side?

Emotions (you know this better
than anyone) are fickle, they swap shapes fast
as the gods. It makes you laugh,
thinking of the hurricanes, all the agonizing waves

he'll learn to endure, enjoy even,
as long as he believes you have a use for him.
The truly fucked are those
for whom obsession never wavers, or self-reflects:

I foundered once so far along that sea
Poseidon had to rescue me himself;
on his temple wall, my sailor's vest still hangs,
shrunken, and to this day somewhat damp.

PETITION

Goddess of physical mail
and a crow's garbage-heap luck,

descend, come whirling
on your bright chariot back

to jackhammer me full
just once more of your fine spunk,

so each line might arrive
bristling with rhyme and intact;

consider, furthermore,
sticking around a little beyond your five

customary minutes;
why this need, good lady,

to withdraw so abruptly,
leaving me alone here again

with mostly dead men
at someone's sick idea of a party?

THE GLADIATOR

His mirrored sunglasses a kind of silence,
his silence its own impermeable pride.
Croquet stakes stubble the yard where he works,
campfire-scars of small gardens gone wrong.
Between his mother's shed and the sidewalk fence
lies the circle of dead grass he stalks
every afternoon, gazing up and around

as if freshly hurled onto the sand of Gérôme's Colosseum.
He first selects a sawed-off golf club
from their wooden stand, wrapping it behind
his rippling shoulders, then, as the sitar music picks up
from his boom box, charms the metal stick
down one arm like a rigid snake.
Slow swoops towards Warrior II
tame whatever rage he might have transferred
onto his instrument, or it to him.

Across the street, the side door of the Contois Tavern
jiggers finally open onto fall cold:
halftime, the Jets game already out of hand.
Propped against the brick, led back
to themselves again, the regulars try not to stare
through their smoke, their low lack of talk,
scuffing falling butt ends like moths
as the gladiator stiffens, thrown from his obscurity—
then whirls, club head flashing, and lunges again.

TWENTY-SOMETHING

Detach from happiness
its myth of choice—and still,

out of some hole in the will,

choice clambers back,
shies near, insinuates itself

between us like a damaged animal,

mouth wide, expecting equally
to be fed or struck.

TRAIL

Won from sand,
an hourglass of the wind
wobbles and rises,
from Shaker dance
to whirling Dervish,
faint sleeve riddled with time

at the Atlantic's limit.
Something in the spindrift
remembers the way, last January,
out of a dog's unleashed
lurch towards objects pungent,
sunk, pink snow would kick up

and, following that mist
as it bent and flexed
thinly on itself, I could think only
of the trail of down,
hidden by winter layers,
along your belly skin,
so palpable in its distance

like this visibly writhing wind.

TRUE LOVE

Off rows of windshields
in the Amtrak lot
rain in sudden
clumps like jacks. Parked cars
with people in them
awaiting people they imagine
hurtling through suburbs
of silver woods
awaiting them. True
love needs interference,
a certain blizzard distance,
for the words to worm through.
Remember Iowa?
Late summer storms that would self-spark
as if our fights could trip
the finest wire beneath the sidewalk.
And the sunlight, harder after.

SQUIRRELS

Something blurred, warmed
in the eye's corner, like woodsmoke
becoming tears;
but when you turned to look

the stoop was still, the pumpkin
and tacky mum pot wouldn't talk—
just a rattle
at the gutter and a sense

of curtains, somewhere, pulled.
Five of them later, scarfing the oak's
black bole,
laying a dream of snakes.

Needy and reticent
at once, these squirrels in charred November
recall, in Virgil,
what it is to feel:

moods, half moods,
swarming, then darting loose; obscure
hunches that refuse
to speak, but still expect

in some flash of luck
to be revealed. The less you try
to notice them,
the more they will know of you.

MERCY

Its water-torture-slow
wend in me. Its work

like the reverse of work.
No wonder human

praise won't stick.
No wonder anger's

more often summoned,
its hum, ready-made,

that steadies my head
like hospital television,

throwing blue rumor
for hours at no one.

OBSERVER

Not seeing me, not even looking,
K. on her silver cruiser charms her way

through the last long moment
of the changing light:

snow boots and a Seychelles Warbler's
old blue tights,

a rolled-up yoga mat in her basket
wobbling like a wild tiller as she pedals.

It feels illicit and somewhat right
to stand across the intersection

without shouting
her name, or even waving.

According to the Internet
tutorial, the fact that photons

turn into tiny loyal billiard balls
as soon as we start watching suggests

no error of method
or measurement, but rather,

as far as anyone can tell,
an invisibly unstable world,

a shaking everywhere
that seeing must pin down and fix.

So, that morning I stumbled on you
out, alone, bending through

the traffic at Orange and Edwards Streets:
a someone else then

whom I, alone,
can never otherwise see—

there has to be a kind of speech
beyond naming, or even praise,

a discipline
that locates light and lets it go.